I Am Respectful

By Kurt Joseph

Gareth Stevens
Publishing

Please visit our Web site, www.garethstevens.com. For a free color catalog of all our high-quality books, call toll free 1-800-542-2595 or fax 1-877-542-2596.

Library of Congress Cataloging-in-Publication Data

Joseph, Kurt.
 I am respectful / Kurt Joseph.
   p. cm. — (Kids of character)
 Includes index.
 ISBN 978-1-4339-4875-6 (pbk.)
 ISBN 978-1-4339-4876-3 (6-pack)
 ISBN 978-1-4339-4874-9 (library binding)
 1. Respect for persons–Juvenile literature. 2. Respect–Juvenile literature. 3. Children–Conduct of life–Juvenile literature.
 I. Title.
 BJ1533.R42J67 2011
 179'.9–dc22
                                           2010036897

First Edition

Published in 2011 by
Gareth Stevens Publishing
111 East 14th Street, Suite 349
New York, NY 10003

Editor: Mary Ann Hoffman
Designer: Christopher Logan

Photo credits: Cover, pp. 1, 15, 21 Shutterstock.com; pp. 5, 11 Stockbyte/Thinkstock; p. 7 iStockphoto/Thinkstock; p. 9 Creatas Images/Thinkstock; p. 13 Hemera/Thinkstock; p. 17 Comstock Images/Thinkstock; p. 19 Getty Images.

Printed in the United States of America

CPSIA compliance information: Batch #CW11GS: For further information contact Gareth Stevens, New York, New York at 1-800-542-2595.

Table of Contents

Boldface words appear in the glossary.

A Respectful Person

A respectful person treats others the way they want to be treated. They use good **manners**. A respectful person accepts differences in people and how they do things.

In the Neighborhood

Abby walked up to the store. A woman was coming into the store at the same time. Abby held the door for her. Abby was respectful.

Pam was at the **library**. She wanted to tell her friend something. Pam used a quiet voice so she would not bother other people. Pam is respectful.

Tim's neighbor planted a new **lawn**. Tim was riding his bike. He was careful to stay on the sidewalk and not ride on the neighbor's lawn. Tim is respectful.

At School

A man came to John's classroom to talk to the students about his job. John waited until the man finished talking before he asked a question. John is respectful.

Tess likes to learn new things in school. Sometimes, her teacher asks the class to work quietly. Tess does not talk to her friends. Tess is respectful.

At Home

Lori's sister bought a new book. She let Lori read it. Lori was careful to take good care of the book. Lori is respectful.

Mark's mother had just washed the floor. Mark's shoes were dirty from playing outside. Mark took his shoes off at the door. He did not get mud on the floor. Mark is respectful.

Ella's parents were talking. Ella wanted to ask them a question. She did not **interrupt**. She waited until they finished talking. Ella is respectful.

Glossary

interrupt: to talk when someone else is talking

lawn: grass

library: a building that has a lot of books

manners: a polite way of acting

For More Information

Books

Suen, Anastasia. *Show Some Respect*. Edina, MN: Magic Wagon, 2008

Thomas, Pat. *Everyone Matters: A First Look at Respect for Others*. Hauppauge, NY: Barron's Educational Series, 2010.

Web Sites

Planet Protectors
http://www.epa.gov/epawaste/education/kids/ planetprotectors/index.htm
Play games and learn how to respect the Earth.

How to Be Respectful
www.goodcharacter.com/pp/respect.html
Use an activity to help understand respect.

Index